THE BEEZER BOOK

Printed and Published in Great Britain by D. C. THOMSON & CO., LTD.,
185 Fleet Street, London EC4A 2HS.
© D. C. THOMSON & CO., LTD., 1989.
ISBN 0-85116-450-1

OPEN UP!

Arf-arf! Welcome to the thirty-third BEEZER BOOK. As you can see, it's the height of good taste!

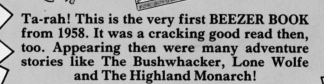

BLAST FROM THE PAST

Ta-rah! This is the very first BEEZER BOOK from 1958. It was a cracking good read then, too. Appearing then were many adventure stories like The Bushwhacker, Lone Wolfe and The Highland Monarch!

101 things to do with your **BEEZER BOOK.**

Improve your balance!

TRIVIA QUIZ

1. *How good are The Badd Lads at dancing?*
2. *Which famous Beezer lived in Roman times?*
3. *What does Mo need wallpaper for?*

The Badd Lads have stolen the answers! You'll have to READ ON for the answers!

THE BANANA BUNCH

I'M PUTTING ON A MAGIC ACT AT THE THEATRE TONIGHT — BUT I'VE GOT BUTTERFLIES IN MY TUMMY.

THEATRE

BRAIN DEPT.

THIS'LL TAKE CARE OF HIS PROBLEM.

HAVE A BIG MEAL!

SUGGESTION BOX

So —

MAYBE SOMETHING TO EAT WILL STILL MY NERVES. I'LL HAVE A SALAD.

GONE TO LUNCH

Soon —

HM! IT DOESN'T LOOK VERY TASTY, BUT I'LL GIVE IT A TRY.

STOP!

And —

Do you have NUMSKULLS!?

READERS—TO FIND OUT IF *YOU* HAVE NUMSKULLS, TRY THIS SIMPLE QUIZ. ANSWER A OR B OR C, TO EACH QUESTION, THEN CHECK YOUR SCORE AT THE BOTTOM OF THE PAGE.

Q 1. DO YOU GET THUMPING HEADACHES?
(a.) NEVER.
(b.) ONCE WITH THE 'FLU.
(c.) 3 O'CLOCK EVERY SATURDAY.

Q 2. DO YOU GET BAD DREAMS?
(a.) NEVER.
(b.) DREAMED ONCE YOU LOST 5p.
(c.) EVERY FRIDAY NIGHT.

Q 3. DO YOU GET NOSE BLEEDS?
(a.) NEVER.
(b.) ONCE, IN A FIGHT.
(c.) EVERY SUNDAY DINNERTIME.

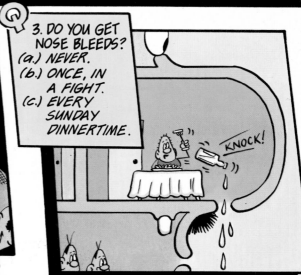

KNOCK!

Q 4. DO YOU GET BURNING FEELINGS ON YOUR TONGUE?
(a.) NEVER.
(b.) WHEN YOU EAT CURRIES.
(c.) EACH NOVEMBER THE 5th.

ANSWERS

SCORE '0' POINTS FOR AN 'A' ANSWER.
SCORE '4' POINTS FOR A 'B' ANSWER.
SCORE '732' POINTS FOR A 'C' ANSWER.

* IF YOU SCORE '0'— SORRY! YOU'VE NOTHING AT ALL IN YOUR HEAD! * IF YOU SCORED '4'— YAWN! YOU'RE SO NORMAL YOU'RE A BIT BORING! * IF YOU SCORED '2,928'— CONGRATULATIONS! YOU'VE A HEAD FULL OF NUMSKULLS!

WE'LL NEVER FIND HIM. EVERYBODY'S GOT GINGER HAIR.

YIKES!

Back home—

GUESS WHAT THE LATEST CRAZE IS, DAD.

OH! I SEE YOU ALREADY KNOW!

Outside—

THERE'S A NEW CRAZE!

GET THAT GINGER WIG OFF. EVERYBODY'S BALANCING WELLIES ON THEIR NOSES.

OW!

THEY ALMOST SCALPED ME! I HOPE THE NEXT CRAZE IS FOR BALD HEADS.

I'M THE MOST FAMOUS BEE AROUND. THINK I'LL DISH OUT SOME AUTOGRAPHS!

In an orchard —

THIS'LL 'BEE' A WORK OF ART.

COO! THAT'S A FUNNY NAME FOR AN APPLE!

Next —

WATCH THIS!

RAT-A-TAT-A-TAT!

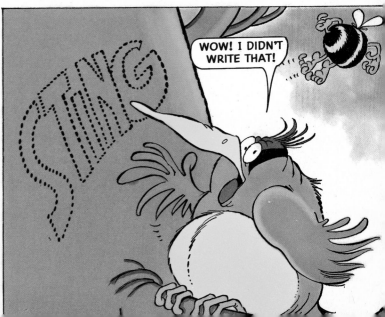

WOW! I DIDN'T WRITE THAT!

Then—

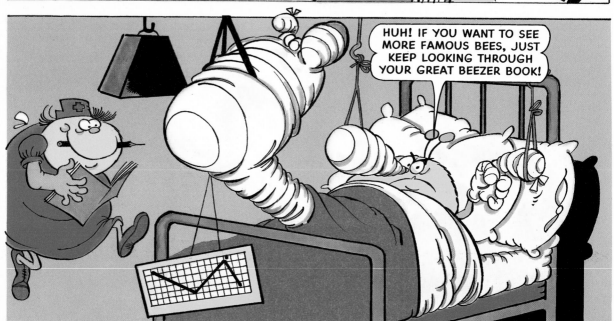

THE BADD LADS

Meanwhile, back at the nick—

YAWN! IT'S NOT THE SAME WITHOUT THE LADS!

BANG! BANG!

WHO'S THUMPING AT OUR GATE?

IF IT'S A DOUBLE GLAZING SALESMAN— THE PRISON'S GOT SOME!

CACKLE! WE'RE TOO FAST FOR 'EM!

HA-HA!

GROAN!

IT'S US! PLEASE TAKE US BACK! WE CAN'T STAND THESE GRANS!

HEALTHY

GROVEL

BOW

CLUB 5

BEEZER

1. Ginger's on holiday in Spain and would like to try some seafood. Can you unscramble the names of the items on the menu?

MENU
BOLSTER ...
STUCOPO ..
DIQUS .....
KRASH.....
TORESSY...
CARLEMKE .
WARPSN ....
MANSOL....

2. At first glance all those hats look the same to Little Mo — but only TWO are. Which two?

1   2   3

4   5   6

7   8   9

4. Sonny and Sandi have hidden 10 sets of false teeth. See if you can find them.

3. Can you insert the letter 'E' 15 times in the sentence below to see what the Beezers are up to?

VRYBWSSMSVRYKNTOSTALICCRAM.

8. Brainy has collected 4 times as many shells as Dopey who has 3 more than Tiny. Lanky has 5 less than Brainy and Fatty has 8 more than Lanky. If Dopey has collected 12 shells, how many have the Banana Bunch collected altogether?

TEEZERS

KITE

BALL

6. *Baby Crockett would rather have a ball than a kite. Turn KITE to BALL in four stages by changing one letter each time to make a new word.*

7. *Who has hooked the treasure chest?*

5. *Colonel Blink wants to go water-skiing but there are 6 things wrong with this little scene. What are they?*

PORKY

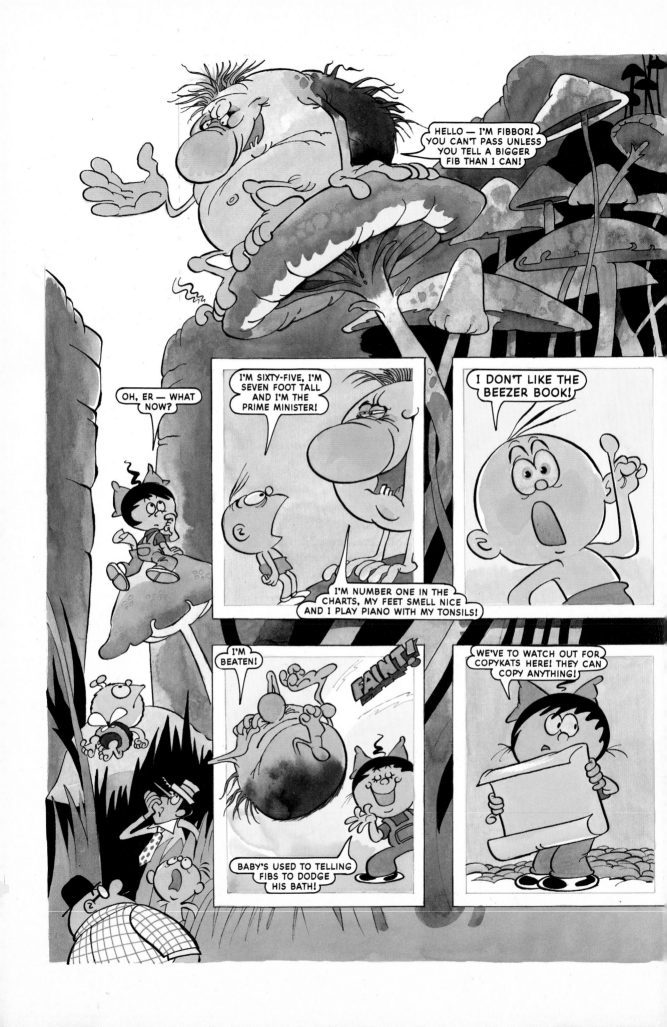

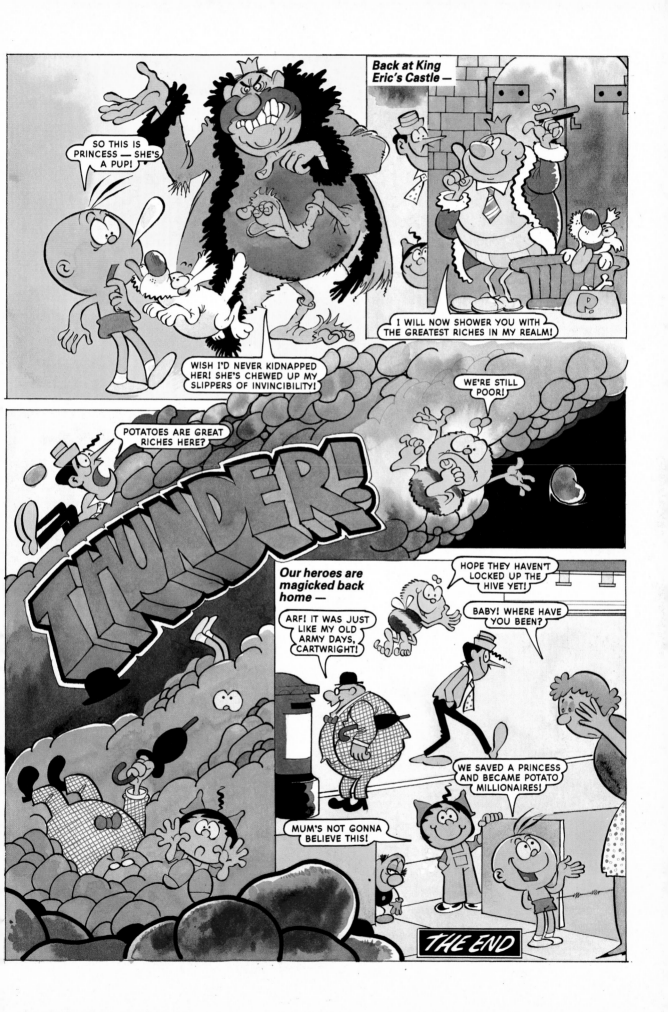

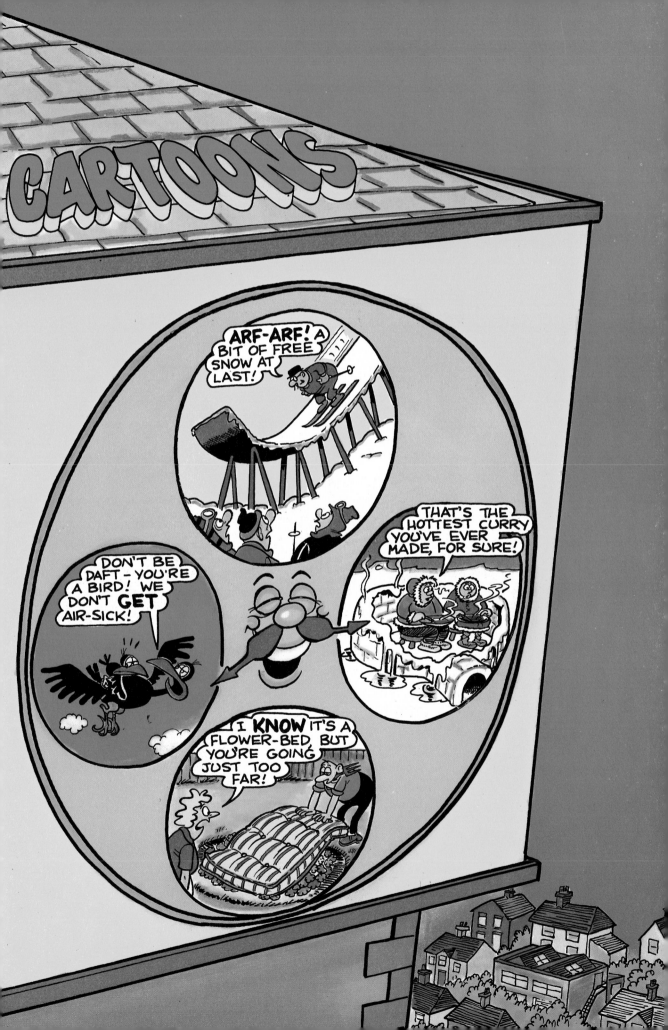

GREAT BEEZ IN HISTORY

HERE'S BLACKBEERD, THE MOST FEARED PIRATE ON THE SEVEN SEAS. HE WAS SO TOUGH, HE WOULD TIE BURNING STICKS IN HIS BEARD TO MAKE HIM EVEN FIERCER — AND HE NEVER WASHED HIS HANDS AT TEA-TIME!

Twitt Hall

YOUNG SID

"THE COPPER'S KID"

TUFF-AND-TINY

I'M GOING TO TELL YOU WHAT IT'S BEEN LIKE HAVING TUFF FOR A PET ALL THIS TIME.

I found him in a cave.

MUMMY!

It was as a baby that he first showed signs of nervousness.

RATTLE! RATTLE! RATTLE!

ER ... CAN YOU STOP RATTLING THAT THING SO LOUDLY?

By the time he was a toddler, it was obvious we were going to have problems with him.

STOP! WE'RE GOING TOO FAST!

EH? UPHILL?

The NUMSKULLS

HUH! I BET AN OLD FOGEY LIKE YOU COULDN'T DO THAT!

ER — OF COURSE I COULD!

OUR MAN COULD INJURE HIMSELF IF HE TRIED THAT. I'LL TELL HIM TO MAKE AN EXCUSE.

I'VE GOT A BAD KNEE

SUGGESTION BOX

So —

I'VE GOT A BAD KNEE JUST NOW!

YAAGH! I DON'T BELIEVE YOU! RASP!

RASP!

NEITHER DO WE!

WE'LL FIND OUT IF HE'S FAKING OR NOT.

EEK! WHAT ARE YOU DOING HERE?

YAH! BOO! WHAT A BUNCH OF COWARDS.

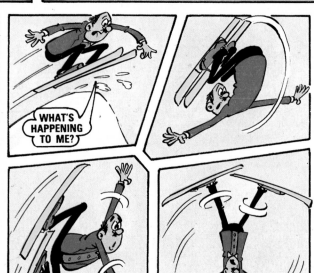

ME AND SOPHIA ARE GOING TO BE NICE TO EACH OTHER AND SHARE A PICNIC ON THE BEACH!

IT'S SILLY, FIGHTING ALL THE TIME!

IT'S JUST A PITY MORE PEOPLE WEREN'T LIKE US! LOOK! HE'S JUST PUNCHED HER!

BOO!

HISS!

LEAVE THAT OLD LADY ALONE, YOU BIG-NOSED BULLY!

OLD, AM I?

OOW! BIG-NOSED, EH?

TAKE THAT! THAT'S THE WAY TO DO IT!

OOYAH!

NAUGHTY! NAUGHTY! NAUGHTY!

OOW!

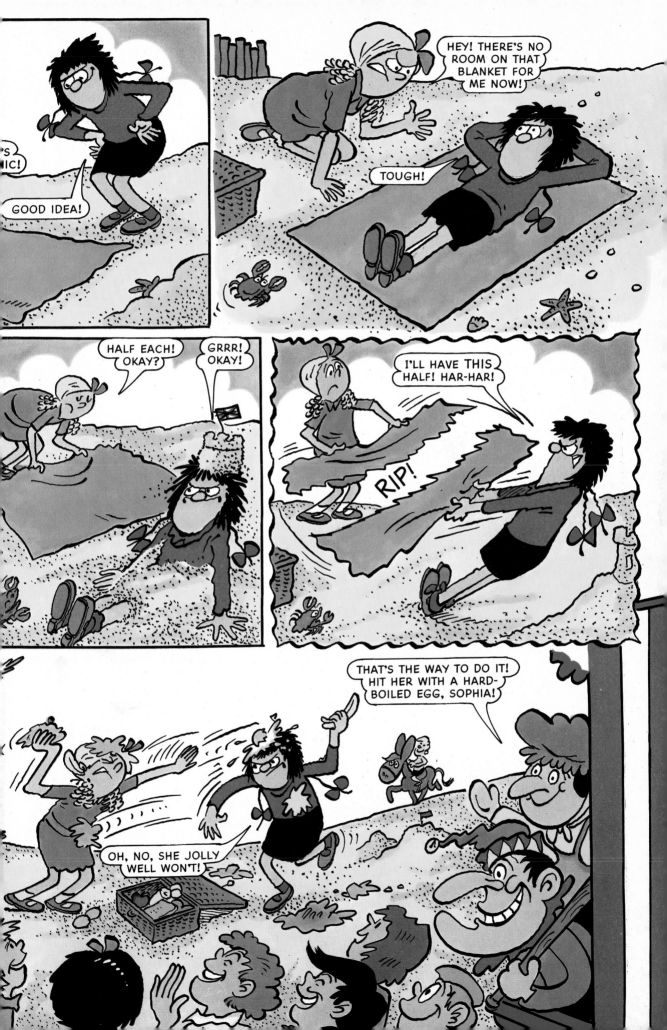

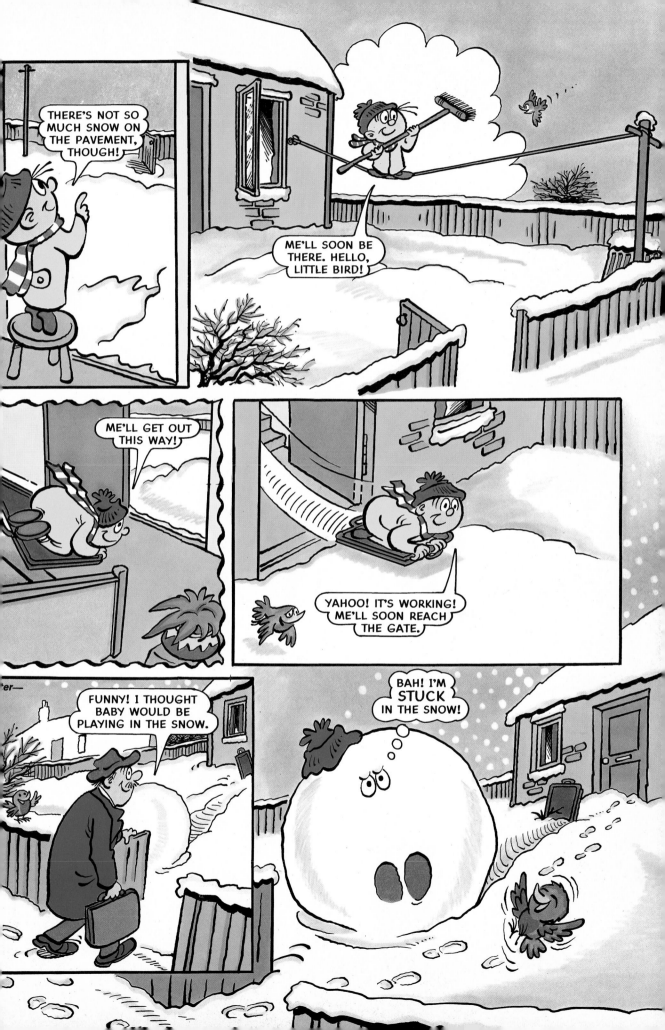

...AND LAST THING AT NIGHT!

500 LINES.
I MUST NOT
GIVE TEACHER
APPLES WITH
BIG WORMS
IN THEM

Z

GONE TO THE DISCO